Happiness at Work

Enhancing Employee Happiness at the Harry Jerome Community Centre during Times of
Organizational Change

By

Jennifer Folkersen

Royal Roads University

An Engaged Leadership Project in partial fulfillment of the requirements for the degree of

Master of Arts

In

Leadership

We accept this Final Report as conforming

To the required standard

David Whittington, PhD, Academic Supervisor

Catherine Etmanski, PhD, School Director

Royal Roads University

August 2018

©Jennifer Folkersen, 2018

Executive Summary

The purpose of this research study was to examine the current level of employee happiness at the Harry Jerome Community Centre within the North Vancouver Recreation and Culture Commission and to discover how employee happiness relates to organizational change. Harry Jerome Community Centre is set within the City of North Vancouver and hosts a swimming pool, ice rink, dedicated youth spaces, fitness centres, sport gymnasiums and multipurpose spaces.

The North Vancouver Recreation and Culture Commission (NVRC) is a partnership between the City and District of North Vancouver which is responsible for providing meaningful recreation and culture opportunities for North Shore Residents (North Vancouver Recreation Commission, 2018). The NVRC serves a diverse, vibrant population of over 52,000 residents in the City (City of North Vancouver, 2018) and over 85,000 in the District of North Vancouver (Statistics Canada, 2016). Of which, Harry Jerome Community Centre is one of 10 Community Centres currently located in the City of North Vancouver (North Vancouver Recreation Commission, 2018).

This project was focussed on the staff team at the Harry Jerome Community Centre but is of a benefit NVRC Commission wide. The community is rapidly changing, and NVRC is adapting, with these changes, staff need to be able to respond happily, productively and for the best of the organization. Because of this, I wanted to create a project that was fundamentally designed by those who would be impacted the most. "Participation not only builds commitment. It ensures everybody learns essential things they did not know" (Weisbord, 2012, p. 204).

Research data was collected through a series of one on one interviews and a ½ day design thinking Happiness Summit. Participants were taken through a series of exercises from IDEO's (2015) Field Guide to Human Centered Design of Inspiration, Ideation and Implementation. Exercises included a collage exercise, Top 5 themes, brainstorming, bundling and a dotmocracy to select the top 3 solutions to the research question. The data was transcribed and analyzed, and findings revealed 5 themes in relation to the research question of how to enhance participants happiness during times of change. The themes represented were; improved systems, relationship building, teamwork, communication and positive leadership.

Within the context of enhancing and supporting employee happiness during times of change, participants had the opportunity to go through a series of exercises to design solutions to meet their unique needs. Solutions were designed by participants and recommendations to these solutions were created by the researcher. Solution 1 included; more time for working with staff with less wasted resources and realistic time frames. The recommendation: to create a task force responsible to review organizational flow, block off time for staff to connect with their teams and create a yearly project calendar. Solution 2; was to put fun into training sessions and celebrate how far the team has come. The recommendation: to include one fun activity into each biweekly meeting, create a monthly social gathering to celebrate recognition and milestones, put fun into in-services and training opportunities by stepping outside of the box, incorporate themes and/or include games as ways to learn. Solution 3; was to create a support system, have staff set daily goals and work together on tasks. The recommendation: to connect back to recent NVRC customer experience coaching and leadership training to incorporate a team to lead this mentorship group.

References

City of North Vancouver. (2018). Retrieved from
        https://www.cnv.org/your-government/about-the-city/community-statistics

North Vancouver Recreation Commission. (2018). *about us*. Retrieved from NVRC:
        https://www.nvrc.ca/about-us

Weisbord, M. R. (2012). *Productive Workplaces; Dignity, meaning, and community in the 21st century*. San Francisco: Jossey-Bass

Acknowledgements

In writing this engaged leadership project I have come to have a better understanding of the connection between employee happiness, organizational success and change. Communities are changing rapidly, and organizations are adapting, employees need to be on board to make these changes successful. To do this, we must take into account, the hearts and minds of our teams, we must engage them in the process and include them, at all levels. This project focussed solely on recreation, however this type of leadership spans to benefit all organizations who are adapting quickly to a changing landscape.

This project would not have been possible without the help of my faculty advisor, Dave Whittington and my pod, James Arden, James Roger, John Eivindson and Lori Stevenson. Thank you for the countless emails and support over the last few months.

I would like to thank my husband Ken Folkersen and our children, Isla and Kai for their undying support through this process. There were many days, hours and months spent behind a computer when I needed quiet time, which they respected. My parents, Bob and Flo Baillie made this education journey and dream possible for me, not only believing in me, but helping with our children whenever we needed it. My appreciation and love for them is infinite.

A special thank you to Royal Roads University and the North Vancouver Recreation and Culture Commission, especially the team at the Harry Jerome Community Centre for all of their effort, and for giving me the opportunity to lead and learn.

Table of Contents

Focus and Framing

The goal of this research project was two-fold: First, to identify the current level of employee happiness at the Harry Jerome Recreation Centre, operated by the North Vancouver Recreation and Culture Commission (NVRC) and second, to have the group define complex solutions to the research question of how we support and enhance employee happiness during times of change.

The NVRC is a partnership between the City of North Vancouver and the District of North Vancouver. "Our mission is to build healthy individuals, families and communities and we know that recreation and culture are vital to the overall health, wellness and creativity of our community" (North Vancouver Recreation Commission, 2018). The NVRC currently operates 10 Community Recreation Centres, with three new centres in various stages of design and build, a tennis centre and a performing arts theatre (North Vancouver Recreation Commission, 2018). They also manage field and facility rentals and outdoor spaces across the North Shore.

The staff at the Harry Jerome Community Centre oversee programs and services that occur at three facilities. The Harry Jerome Community Centre, Mickey McDougal Gym and Memorial Gym. Amongst these facilities are 3 gymnasiums, a swimming pool, arts and crafts rooms, a spin studio, three weight rooms, a designated cardiac fitness centre, a childcare centre, a yoga studio and various multipurpose spaces.

There is no one definition of recreation, however all references found relate to the essential nature of doing something for the sole sake of enjoyment and pleasure often working with others while learning new skills. Aristotle argued in the *Nichomachean Ethics,* "leisure is more important than work because leisure provides pleasure and happiness in life" (as cited in Newman, Tay, & Diener, 2013). There is an organizational culture when working in recreation that supports and celebrates employee leisure opportunities for both employees and their families. It would be similar to be a coffee connoisseur while working in a fantastic coffee shop, enjoying all the benefits of which one loves. Recreation staff are often drawn to this line of work because of their own positive personal experiences in the arts, sports, or fitness. James Arden, Director of Park Services for the City of Abbotsford said that he was drawn to a career in recreation because it allowed him to provide space for people to choose how to spend their leisure time (J. Arden, personal communication, August 14, 2018).

NVRC offers their employees a great work/life balance through flexible work schedules, an earned day off program, great medical benefits, free swimming, skating and fitness passes, and discounts on registered programs. The combination of a flexible work environment, meaningful interesting work and great benefits have made this a desirable organization to work for. These benefits encourage employees to stay connected to their community through recreation and leisure opportunities.

Relevant Literature

This literature review includes relevant academic literature that expands on aspects of employee happiness and organizational change that is relevant to this study. Certain aspects of this literature review will ultimately inform and direct the conclusions and recommendations.

Achor (2012) looked at ways individuals can cultivate their own sense of well-being and set themselves up to succeed. He indicated that employee happiness relates to a sense of well-being and personal responsibility. His research also points out the importance of happy employees and the bottom line. Employees who score low in "life satisfaction" stay home on average 1.25 more times per month equaling about 15 days per year than their happier counterparts. Happier employees are also more likely to receive higher ratings from customers. Most recreation staff are front line staff who directly serve the community in various ways, through programs and essential services. By increasing their "life satisfaction", we will directly impact the community we serve, and the organization's bottom line in a positive way.

Boehm and Lyubormirsky (2008) argued that happiness correlates with workplace success and positive affect leads to improved workplace outcomes similarly to Achor (2012). Their research looked at the question of "does happiness promote career success or does career success promote happiness". Similar to the article listed above, "Positive Intelligence", this article stated that "compared to less happy peers, happy people earn more money, display superior performance and perform more helpful acts" (p.101). That being said, happiness can not be found in every circumstance, Boehm and Lyubomirsky (2008), found that people should experience a healthy balance of both positive and negative emotions. Cropanzano and Wright (2001) looked at the ambiguity of the happy-productive worker thesis and suggested a fulsome health approach to promote better performance. Their research indicated, that happier workers tend to be able to afford to take more risks at work than less happy workers as they have a higher reserve of happiness.

Fisher (2010), argued that happiness is one of the most sought after values in society and that "joy appears in every topography of basic human emotions" (p. 384). She wrote that workplace happiness is much more than job satisfaction but related to different constructs in the workplace including transient, person and unit level. The transient level, related to short term moods and emotions individuals may experience. The person level, related to the different levels of happiness experienced between people, and the unit level related to teams, organizations and measures of happiness amongst these groups. This relates to Scott's (n.d.) article which discussed the importance of happiness at work and related significant positive outcomes of experiencing happiness at work including the importance of employment status, job type and workplace characteristics and how these relate to measures of subjective well being, as well global wellbeing. To further convey this theory, Scott (n.d.) indicated that happiness can help to shape job market outcomes and performance through job characteristics. They pondered the question, "What makes for a good job?" and what aspects are most predictive of workplace wellness. What is important beyond income? Across the board, the strongest predictor of workplace happiness was work-life balance. Careers in recreation lend themselves to flexible work environments which capitalize on work-life balance.

Ergle (2015), researched the rise of employee engagement through games or gamification to increase organizational success and team happiness. This is a fairly new approach, however in my research, participants stated they wanted to experience more fun in training and in-services, gamification could be the solution to enhance engagement throughout NVRC. The researcher used design thinking to create prototypes and employees were encouraged to join teams to develop the ideas and pitch them in a 'shark tank' type of way, creating friendly competition and engagement. The article also discussed the millennials and future generations who are used to using technology in a way that accesses competition.

Grant, Christianson and Price (2007), research highlighted the effects of managerial practices on employee well-being and offered guidelines for managing and mitigating well-being tradeoffs. Similarly, this report suggested that current research shows the impact employee well-being has on job performance, and overall organizational success. The author suggested there are three important core dimensions of employee well-being; social, psychological and physical. Employee well-being is complex and multi-faceted, and for organizations to see benefits, managerial practices must be framed within the context of employee well-being and happiness.

Mafini and Dlodlo (2014), looked at four extrinsic motivation factors; remuneration, quality of work life, supervision and teamwork and found that the relationship with promotion was insignificant, but a significant relationship was established with life satisfaction. Shaheen, and Mohanty, (2017) discussed how engaged employees are positive and efficacious and investigated how these employees delighted their patients. The article also looked at the perception from the employees on the impact of their efforts on their patients. They found work engagement predicted a higher psychological capital which in turn affected customer delight. Having a high life satisfaction indicator would then result in higher engagement at work which would then provide more positive experiences to customers and/or patients.

Taris and Schreurs, (2009) supported the theory that happy organizations are productive organizations and they correlated relationships amongst levels of demand, control, support, emotional exhaustion and satisfaction against performance. The findings from this study suggested the average level of employee burnout/emotional exhaustion in the organization mattered for overall organizational performance. Similarly, this was reported in the Happiness Summit and Interviews as participants stated they felt unhappy when there were tight timelines, communication breakdowns and gossip amongst the team. These factors relate to Taris and Schreurs's (2009) theory of how emotional exhaustion affect performance. Participants of the Happiness Summit indicated that negative interactions and unexpected assignments affected their emotional state which in turn, as per Taris and Schreurs (2009) research affected performance. Wright and Cropanzano (2007) moderated the relationship between psychological well-being, job satisfaction and job performance. Their research provided similar evidence to the articles above and states that job performance was highest when employees reported scores in both personal well-being and job satisfaction.

Significance of the Project

As mentioned above, the purpose of my capstone project was to examine the level of employee happiness at the Harry Jerome Community Centre and seek ways to enhance and support happiness while employees experience organizational changes. By understanding the importance of employee happiness, and how this level of happiness is affected by organizational change, we have the opportunity to mitigate the negative impacts for the wellbeing of our employees. "Being happy at work is a fundamental element of a person's life satisfaction" (Diane E. Scott, n.d.). Boehm and Lyubomirsky (2008), wrote that happiness is aligned with success in the workplace and there is evidence to suggest that "…happiness often precedes measures of success and that induction of positive affect leads to improved workplace outcomes" (p. 101). This is an important topic to explore as there are major organizational change projects on the horizon within the North Vancouver Recreation and Culture Commission, specifically Harry Jerome Community Centre, and these changes may challenge employee happiness. This research project is an opportunity to provide solutions and recommendations to enhance employee happiness before these major organizational changes take place. The solutions were designed by participants who have a vested interest in the outcomes of this project.

I focussed my research on the Harry Jerome Community Centre staff team because I wanted the project to be of a direct benefit to the team, of which I am part of. I am a Recreation Program Coordinator responsible for sports, youth and fitness programs at three facilities within the Harry Jerome Recreation complex, and I am familiar with major organizational changes the staff will be experiencing in the next few years. Participants of this research study, consisted of program coordinators, administrative supervisory staff, fitness and aquatic staff. These participants oversee many different program areas including fitness, sports, childcare, arts and culture, aquatics, adapted programs, access programs, child, youth and seniors programs, and front desk administrative duties. Being part of the Harry Jerome team has provided greater insight into upcoming changes and the unique needs of the staff team. Not only are there large organizational changes in the future, the City is changing rapidly to adapt.

The Harry Jerome Community Centre is in the City of North Vancouver. In 2016, the population reached 52.898, and for the period of 2011 – 2016 the City's population has grown by 9.3% annually (City of North Vancouver, 2018). The community centre serves a vibrant, diverse population in an area of ongoing economic development. The increase in development has highlighted the need for more programs and services, as well a need to replace an aging facility

to meet the needs of the changing community. Because the City of North Vancouver is growing

and changing so rapidly, I was interested to know if the impact would affect employee happiness

while at work. According to Grant, Christianson and Price (2007), "extensive evidence indicates

that employee well-being has a significant impact on the performance and survival of

organizations by affecting costs related to illness and health care" (p. 51). Keeping employees

happy, healthy and productive at work will help to mitigate negative impacts the organization

may experience while going through major organizational changes. While the City is growing

at a rapid rate, it is important for NVRC to recognize the impacts of this growth on the staff

team. With major changes on the horizon, it is vitally important to have an engaged staff team as

the ambassadors of change for NVRC.

Harry Jerome has three major upcoming changes; a new registration software system, a

new megacomplex facility and a fitness service review. Stroh (2015), argued to build a

foundation of change, one must engage key stakeholders, establish common ground, build

collaborative capacity and close the loop. That being said, Weisbord (2012), through his

research, discussed the fundamental importance for the greatest potential of growth and change,

must be developed through collective responsibility, learning and action. I believe my research

offered that opportunity to the participants and this will help to develop internal strategies to

increase the level of engagement and overall happiness of the Harry Jerome Recreation staff

team. These strategies will cultivate a sense of well-being amongst the team which will support

them through these major changes. The human-centered design approach to the research will have a collective impact that will benefit the current and future staff of the Harry Jerome Community Centre and the NVRC.

This project will benefit the NVRC by creating a positive, supportive working environment with solutions created directly by the people who will be impacted by a variety of organizational changes the most. Using an innovative, human centered design approach to the research, participants engaged in a thoughtful process which led them to a have a deeper understanding of their teams' values, wants and needs. This approach aligned the teams vision to see what their potential to discover could be. Senge (1990) wrote, "A shared vision, especially one that is intrinsic, uplifts people's aspirations. Work becomes part of pursuing a larger purpose embodied in the organization's' products or services" (p. 207). It's not only about discovering potential, but also aligning the teams vision as to how they see themselves as part of the process of change.

Engaged Approach

This project was completed using an action-oriented approach to the research. Action-oriented research is an approach to research that informs policy and practice which leads to social change (Small, 1995). According to Small (1995), the focus of action-oriented research has historically evolved. In the past, action research was mainly connected to private industry and organizational development however; recently, scholars with social science disciplines with diverse backgrounds and interests have begun producing this type of research. Rapaport (1970) defined action research as "... aims to contribute both to the practical concerns of people in an immediate problematic situation and to the goals of social science by joint collaboration within a mutually acceptable ethical framework" (as cited in Small, 1995, p. 942). As action research

progresses, focus and methodology may change based on new information surfacing. Because

there are often many contributors involved in action research and they bring their diverse

perspectives and experiences to the study, they must use multiple methods to ensure all

viewpoints are captured and expressed (Small, 1995). This was demonstrated throughout the

Happiness Summit with participants viewpoints changing based on evolving discussions and

questions asked. Action research works to provide the research findings to study participants to

benefit the situation and potentially lead to scientific journal publications, this is a result of the

value of leading social change (Small, 1995). Action research can lead to new learnings and

understandings by providing a multidimensional, holistic, diverse analysis that can be applied to

enact social change. It can be used to further interpret and understand the data collected to solve

a problem and provide recommendations for change. This is an exciting style of research as it

allows one to engage, connect and make a difference resulting in a research based solution to a

problem.

There were two phases to the data collection; The first phase consisted of three individual

interviews and the second phase consisted of a ½ day Happiness Summit. The interviews and

Happiness Summit were planned and completed within a one-week timeframe. Invitations,

information and consent forms were distributed a week prior to the events and I introduced the

project to the participants both in a regular staff meeting and individually one on one.

An important piece of this project was to have the whole team in the room so I could

discover a richer, more diverse perspective within the data. Weisbord (2012) wrote, "Systems

can be improved only to the extent that everyone who works in them understands how they work" (p. 285). The Research Ethics Board needed to assure strict participant safety in the process, so I had to remove a few key players from the data collection, to mitigate any potential 'power over' dynamics. Within this context, I had to remove an employee of a higher level as other employees in similar roles were unable to attend the Summit.

The qualitative interviews consisted of 8 standard questions. The purpose of a qualitative interview is to establish common patterns and themes amongst the data through conversation (Warren, 2001). The questions were; How happy are you generally when you come to work? How would you describe what happiness at work means to you? What are some of the things that affect your happiness at work? When changes happen at work, how does this affect your happiness? Can you tell me about a situation or scenario where you felt really happy at work? What was it about that scenario that increased your level of happiness? Can you tell me about a situation or scenario where you felt less than happy at work? What was it about that scenario that decreased your level of happiness? As participants answered the questions, I let the discussion flow and asked other questions to help clarify their thoughts and feelings. The interviews were all completed prior to the Happiness Summit so I could get a better idea of the current state of affairs.

The Happiness Summit was a ½ day design thinking event and there were a total of 6 employees present for the event. To set the tone for the day, I opened with an introduction of the project and the importance of the team to embrace big ideas. I explained they may experience divergent and convergent thinking processes and if so, were on the right track. I reiterated the explicit expectation of absolute confidentiality throughout the process of the project and welcomed them with a Danish style breakfast to get them in the right frame of mind. I thought this fit well, as Denmark has long been considered one of the happiest Countries in the World as

per the World Happiness Report (Helliwell, Layard, & Sachs, 2018).

My principle inquiry question was posted on the wall for participants to consider and

keep in the forefront of their minds during the Happiness Summit, "How might we enhance and

support employee happiness during times of change?". Sub-questions were not posted, however

included: (a) What changes need to be made to increase your level of happiness at work? (b)

What would you imagine this team would look like if the level of happiness and engagement

increased? (c) What is our potential we still need to discover? (d) How might change affect our

level of happiness at work? (e) What might we create to support our team's happiness at work?

(f) How might stakeholders define the word "happiness"? Sub questions were considered during

the preparation of the interview and Happiness Summit and when analyzing the data.

The Happiness Summit consisted of the three phases of IDEO's (2015) human-centered

design process, Inspiration, Ideation and Implementation. I split the group into two based on

hierarchy and role within the organization to minimize any power over dynamics. For the

Inspiration phase, I placed 100 medium sized collage image cards on the table and asked

participants to pick one picture that described what happiness at work felt like to them. Each

person shared why they picked their card and related it to their feelings of happiness at work.

While each person shared, I had a participant from each group write descriptive words on sticky

notes. I then did the same exercise again, but asked participants to pick one picture that

described how it felt when large organizational changes took effect at work, again one person from each group wrote descriptive words on sticky notes. I asked the groups to post all of their

sticky notes on the wall and report out the results to the larger group.

When the Inspiration phase was completed, we moved into the Ideation phase of the

Summit. I asked each group to review their sticky notes and as a team, sort them into their top 5

emerging themes. The groups worked to categorize their sticky notes by moving them around,

discussing possible themes and finally placing them into their top 5 most important themes.

Based on these themes, I asked each group to brainstorm ways to enhance or support employee

happiness at work during times of change by generating as many ideas they could on sticky notes

during a short time frame. This was an easy task for some group members, and more difficult for

others. I observed some group members struggling to come up with ideas in this phase, so I

reminded them about divergent thinking processes and highlighted the importance of any idea is

a good idea. Once they understood that ideas could be big with outside of the box thinking, they

were able to let the ideas flow. All of the ideas were posted on one wall in combination with the

other groups notes for participants to view. From here, I asked them as a larger group to start

bundling ideas or sticky notes into actionable complex solutions. I advised them to remove any

sticky notes that were not of any service to their solutions. They began layering and combining

individual sticky notes into solutions with 3 or more ideas attached. Once they had bundled as

many ideas as possible, I had one person write these ideas onto flip chart paper and report out to

the group. They produced eight actionable complex solutions to the question of, 'How do we

enhance and support employee happiness during times of change?'.

Moving into the Implementation phase, I gave each person three sticky dots and asked

them to pick their top three solutions of the eight created. The top three solutions needed to be actionable, possible and aligned with their vision of supporting change while enhancing the happiness of the team. To ensure validity of the data, I finished the session by asking each person if they agreed with the top three solutions chosen by the group. The Happiness Summit was made possible by the support of my academic team.

To support my research, my academic supervisor, student POD, advisory and inquiry team helped me work through the process including supporting me to create the original idea of the Happiness Summit, interview questions, the Summit plan, timing and specific exercises and the data member checking and theming. Inquiry team member, Derek Lowe, MAL, helped review, theme and categorize the data from sticky notes and flip charts. The data was captured through audio recording and transcription, flip charts, post it notes and hand-written notes.

ELP Findings, Conclusions, Limitations

ELP Findings

The findings from this research project were determined by participants through a series of exercises. Participants categorized and themed the data based on what would be of a direct benefit to them while navigating happiness and organizational change. To have a better understanding of the findings, I had to determine answers to four baselines questions:

1) How happy are the participants when they come to work

2) What makes them happy

3) What makes them unhappy and

4) How do they describe what change at work feels like based on their experience.

There was a unanimous theme of participants feeling generally happy at work. One participant stated she did not have any fear or anxiety or concern about going to work, she appreciated her job and enjoys going to work on a daily basis. Another participant stated she is 90% happy when she goes to work. Other participants described feelings of happiness through satisfaction of work, feeling like their work is valued, comfort in their roles and having positive interactions with people. Gavin and Mason (2004) emphasized, "when a workplace is designed and managed to create meaning for its workers they tend to be more healthy and happy" (p. 381). Similarity, Denmark's Job Satisfaction Index (2017) listed seven important factors for job satisfaction that closely related to the factors participants of this project indicated; "knowing that your work makes sense, whether you experience having a say, whether you feel fully in charge of your work, the extent that you are generating results, whether you are satisfied with leadership within the workplace, whether you feel good around colleagues, and whether you experience a balance between work life and spare time" (p. 6). There were shared themes of flexibility, autonomy, supportive team, feeling valued, having a positive impact on the community, continuous learning through unexpected challenges, helping and teaching others, increasing other people's happiness and having the support of the team around them. One participant stated her happiness stems from enjoying her coworkers, flexibility in her role and having a supportive supervisor. Another participant stated her happiness comes from doing something positive at work, feeling like she makes a difference through being with and helping people. This relates to Gavin and Mason's (2004) research that organizational happiness is an outcome of meaningful work opportunities. Having understood the current level of employee happiness, it was important to look at stressors that make employees unhappy at work.

Variables that made participants unhappy at work were unexpected tight time constraints, being criticized, not being heard, communication breakdowns and gossip amongst the team. On top of this, an interesting theme emerged from both the interviews and design thinking session of the importance of integrity, knowing that decisions and choices were coming from a good place with no ill intent. Even when an error was made, it was important for coworkers and supervisors to know that it was coming from a place of good intention. One participant relayed, her happiness was affected in a negative way when approached and criticized for work done, when her intentions were good. "Job stress is felt when the demands of the work exceed the workers' belief in their capacity to cope" (Gavin & Mason, 2004, p. 380). Another participant relayed that her happiness was affected mostly when experiencing negative communication with a coworker, which caused her stress. Gavin and Mason (2004) asserted in their research that, "job-specific stressors include long working hours, high workloads, conflicting or ambiguous requests for work to be done, and work versus family conflicts affect productivity and positive experiences at work." (p. 381). Unfavorable intent, difficulty with coworkers and communication issues raise the levels of stress which negatively affect participants happiness at work. Unhappiness coupled with organizational changes can lead to organizational disaster, therefore we needed to look at how organizational changes affect the participants.

Organizational changes have affected the participants in a variety of ways. Most responded that they understood necessary organizational changes and felt as though change could be great and exciting but were often left feeling like there was misdirection and communication breakdowns. One participant said, "It's like there's a brightness at the end of a tunnel, but in the meantime, you're sitting there with a lot of unknown". Another participant noted when change is happening, it makes everything hazy, "We're still trying to do what we do, but we don't know what we're doing".

There were five distinct themes observed from the interview data and the Happiness Summit in response to the research question of how we enhance and support employee happiness during times of change. The five themes were systems, relationship building, teamwork, communication and positive leadership. In the following paragraphs, I will discuss these themes in greater detail.

Systems

Participants expressed the importance of creating more time for working with staff by reducing the amount of administrative time required in their roles. To do this they would have to minimize wasted resources and have realistic working time frames. Changing the current system will take time and effort. Stroh (2015) wrote, "systems thinking motivates people because they discover their role in exacerbating the problems they want to solve" (p. 21).

Systems thinking is best done when "a problem is chronic, diverse stakeholders find it difficult to align their efforts, they try to optimize their part of the system without understanding their impact on the whole, stakeholders short-term efforts undermine their intentions to solve the problem, people are working on a large number of initiatives at the same time, and promoting best practices comes at the expense of engaging in continuous learning" (Stroh, 2015, p. 24).

Participants also highlighted the importance of anticipating retirements through ongoing succession planning. One participant discussed the importance of being proactive in the event of leaves of absences such as retirements and maternity leaves so new staff are fully on board and trained. She emphasized the benefits of up-training for employees and the consequences of pressure and stress this puts on remaining staff, if not done in time.

Relationship Building

Relationship building was an important theme throughout the Happiness Summit and interviews. Participants stated they could build relationships through mentoring co-workers, working to achieve set goals, having weekly get togethers and most importantly celebrating successes. Fisher (2010) wrote, causes of happiness at work are related to environment, circumstance, intrinsic predisposition, and relationships. One participant suggested that it was important to celebrate success while on task, because many times things get started and there's no end point.

Participants stated celebration was an important part of enhancing their happiness and relationships at work. Newstrom (2002), argued that fun at work leads to lower employee anxiety, alleviating feelings of boredom and reducing perceived rates of stress. Participants responded they felt taking time to celebrate how far they have come while going through change was vitally important to their happiness at work.

Team Work

Participants asserted that enjoying their coworkers was one of the most important predictors of their happiness at work. One participant stated, "I know there are people I relate to and enjoy, there is no sort of interpersonal drama in this facility for sure, as far as I know, my coworkers make it a great place to be". Another participant stated, "My team here is amazing". Participants responded by stating that working collaboratively on larger projects for the greater good in a timely manner together was important for their overall happiness at work.

Communication

Participants indicated that there was a need for better communication around rationale for changes. Husain (2013) asserted, "the success of the dissemination and adaptation of organizational change significantly depends upon communicative and informative skills of managers at all levels" (p. 44). Many felt that having ongoing information sessions during change projects would help clarify and create understanding. One participant stated the importance of identifying team and individual fears about change through communication. "Being able to identify any fears at the start, so as we're going through it, we've got somebody that's there to rely on for information".

Positive Leadership

Participants noted it was important for them to walk the talk and model the way for other staff. They appreciated this style of leadership in their current supervisor at the Harry Jerome Community Centre. They felt it was important to create a buddy support system within the workplace and set leadership goals amongst the team. Having all staff on board, including auxiliary staff would also create a lesser feeling of hierarchy.

Conclusions

The findings highlighted five important themes within the data that were required to enhance and support employee happiness while experiencing organizational change. The themes were systems, relationship building, teamwork, communication and positive leadership. These recommendations have been presented to the participants of the study based on their solutions. Going forward, I will work with the Leadership team from the Harry Jerome Community Centre to execute these recommendations.

Within these themes, the participants were able to discover their potential. Through communication and relationship building, they said they wanted transparency and trustworthiness in the process, they wanted the team to understand the importance of the value of integrity, and they wanted to celebrate together. Through positive leadership they want to walk the talk, include all staff (including auxiliary staff), in decisions and create a culture with less hierarchy. Through teamwork they want to mentor and teach each other to increase their skills and enhance their happiness. They acknowledged and shared the importance of having specific systems in place to follow through with these changes.

The participants said that clear communication leads to deeper understanding and predictability during times of change. This is turn enhances how they feel when they are at work and in effect raises their level of happiness in the workplace. They also said the importance of stability through increased communication helps to better understand why change processes are happening a certain way. Being able to identify fears around proposed changes and having the opportunity to align these fears by creating different ideas to move forward would create a positive impact on the team. They imagined that with these changes, they would experience a higher functioning, more cohesive, efficient work team.

Through the exercises presented, the participants designed 8 complex solutions to the research question. The solutions were rated by importance through a dotmocracy exercise. I have listed these in order based on the rating, number 1 being most important to the participants.

1) More time for working with staff with less administrative time. Minimize wasted resources and establish realistic time frames.

2) Put fun into training sessions and celebrate how far we have come.

3) Create a buddy system to have staff work together on tasks and help staff reach goals

4) Walk the talk by challenging the direction

5) Offer clear communication about rationale for changes, ensure we have representation on all types of committees through weekly get togethers, so we can learn together

6) Create less feelings of hierarchy by including all staff (auxiliary) and celebrate together.

7) More direction through the change process, ensure we have an expert in each area of change and be willing to mentor and teach each other

8) Anticipate retirements through succession planning

Limitations

There are several factors that may limit the application of the findings from this research project. Factors include not having the whole system in the room, meaning, not all employees of the Harry Jerome Community Centre were present. There is a large team of staff that work out of this Community Centre whose views, attitudes and opinions were not included because of the ethical implications of the project.

This project was completed with employees who were in similar non-reporting roles to the researcher. The individual interviews were completed with the same employees that attended the Happiness Summit, so this may also limit the information provided to a specific group of people which does not allow us to explore the happiness levels of all employees at the Harry Jerome Community Centre.

Other limitations include the recommendations from the Happiness Summit. The most important recommendation from participants was to have more time for working with staff and less administrative time. To reduce administrative time, there must be better systems in place with more support which may incur budget implications. Other recommendations from the Happiness Summit included having realistic time frames, which are sometimes unavoidable based on the situation.

Recommendations

The Harry Jerome Community Centre team hosts a positive workplace culture. This culture translates to an engaged, happy team and great place to work. Boehm and Lyubomirsky (2008), contended that happiness relates to a variety of workplace outcomes such as personal and organizational success and improved workplace outcomes. Weisbord (2012), argued that people "hunger for community in the workplace" (p. XXXVii). Although participants recognized the positive culture, they indicated there was room for improvement to further enhance their enjoyment on the job.

During the Happiness Summit, participants designed 8 solutions to the research question. I would advise the organization for the purpose of this research project, to focus on working to implement the top 3 solutions provided. These solutions have been listed in order of significance to the participants.

1) More time for working with staff with less wasted resources and realistic time frames.

2) Put fun into training sessions and celebrate how far we have come

3) Create a support system, have staff set daily goals and work together on tasks

My recommendation to implement solution #1, has three parts:

A) Create a task force to look at ways to reduce wasted resources and improve organizational flow, therefore opening up time for staff to work with their teams. Kouzes and Posner (2012) argued, "collaboration is a critical competency for achieving and sustaining high performance". This working group will review current, highly used systems to find and reduce inefficiencies.

B) Block off time for staff to connect with their teams and

C) Create a yearly calendar, so all staff are aware of the major projects and ongoing yearly tasks to be completed to get a head start.

Not only will this solution help to increase job satisfaction amongst the team, it will also improve organizational flow. Looking at tasks and removing, delegating and/or shrinking the unimportant tasks improves productivity and will allow for more time to focus on the desires of the team (Bailey, 2016).

My recommendation to implement solution #2, is to rotate and assign the position of "Fun Seeker" to staff. Owler, Morrison and Plester (2010) found evidence of improved retention, workplace participation, recruitment and employee engagement through the contribution of fun at work. As well, Fluegge (2008), found evidence to suggest that fun at work increases productivity, creates greater employee engagement and is an overall important factor in a job. Fluegge's (2008) research defined fun at work as that which involves, "any social, interpersonal, or task activities at work of a playful or humorous nature which provide an individual with amusement, enjoyment, or pleasure" (p. 15). The recommended rotating position would include three responsibilities:

A) Include one fun activity into each biweekly meeting

B) Create a monthly social gathering to celebrate recognition and milestones

C) Put fun into in-services and training opportunities by stepping outside of the box, incorporating themes and/or including games

My recommendation to implement solution #3, is to connect back to recent NVRC customer experience coaching and leadership training. This training provided tools to coach and mentor staff in a capacity as both the coach and coachee. The training was completed in June, yet there has been no follow up for those interested in pursuing this option. My recommendation within this solution would be to have one interested person from Harry Jerome lead this mentorship team help connect interested individuals. These parties would meet biweekly to work towards their personal goals of achievement. Kouzes and Posner (2012) wrote, "Leaders significantly increase people's belief in their own ability to make a difference. They move from being *in control* to *giving over control* to others. Becoming their coach" (p. 243). This strategy connects back to solution #1, by increasing the time to work with fellow staff members and encouraging deeper more meaningful staff relationships.

Implications

The results of this research project have highlighted implications for positive social change at both the individual and organizational level. The findings highlighted themes of systems, relationship building, teamwork, communication and positive leadership. These themes connected to the conclusions and recommendations the participants designed as to ways to enhance and support employee happiness during times of change. Implementing better systems to reduce inefficient practices, give staff more time to work with one and other. The positive effect of putting fun into training sessions and celebrating more often, will be more staff engagement, teamwork and better working relationships. As well, individuals will be able to provide positive leadership through an ongoing coaching and mentoring program.

NVRC will see the benefits of these changes through higher productively, a more engaged workforce, greater staff retention and most importantly a better understanding of what is required when large changes at work take place.

For the purpose of this research project, I engaged staff within the Harry Jerome Community Centre through the Happiness Summit and interview process, as well the Centre Coordinator, Janet Wallace. They actively engaged and participated in the project and will be looking to implement the recommendations in the near future. To optimize successful implementation of the project, the recommendations will be shared through presentations to senior management and formal reports will be delivered to all participants and stakeholders.

References

Achor, S. (2012). Positive intelligence. *Harvard Business Review*, 100-102.

Bailey, C. (2016). *The productivity project.* Toronto, ON: Random House Canada.

Boehm, J. K., & Lyubomirsky, S. (2008). Does happiness promote career success? *Journal of Career Assessment, 16*, 101-116.

Bushe, G. (2012). Foundations of appreciative inquiry: History, criticism and potential. *AI practitioner*.

City of North Vancouver. (2018). Retrieved from

https://www.cnv.org/your-government/about-the-city/community-statistics

Claypool, K. K. (2017). *Organizational success: How the presence of happiness in the workplace affects employee engagement that leads to organizational success.* Pepperdine University. ProQuest LLC.

Cooperrider, D. L., & Whitney, D. (2005). *Appreciative Inquiry: A positive revolution in change.* Berrett-Koehler Publishers.

Cropanzano, R., & Wright, T. (2001). When a "happy" worker is really a "productive" worker. *Consulting Psychology Journal: Practice and Research, 53*, 182-199.

Diane E. Scott, R. M. (n.d.). *Happiness at work.* Retrieved from Semantic Scholar : https://pdfs.semanticscholar.org/57ad/f01a5fc515225e344cfc22ba04f74779e3c5.pdf

Ergle, D. (2015). Fostering employee engagement through gamification: AirBaltic forecaster

    tool. *Management, 10*, 219-234.

Fisher, C. D. (2010). Happiness at work. *International journal of Management Reviews, 12*,

    384-412.

Fluegge, E. R. (2008). Who put the fun in functional? Fun at work and its effects on job

    performance. Available from ABI/INFORM. Collection; ProQuest Dissertations &

    Theses Global. (193646042). Retrieved from

    https://ezproxy.royalroads.ca/login?url=https://search-proquest-com.ezproxy.royalroads.c

    a/docview/193646042?accountid=8056

Gavin, J. H., & Mason, R. O. (2004). The Virtuous Organization: The value of happiness in the

    workplace. *Organizational Dynamics, 33*, 379-392.

Goleman, D., Boyatzis, R., & McKee, A. (2013). *Primal Leadership.* Boston, Massachusetts:

    Harvard Business Review Press.

Grant, A. M., Christianson, M. K., & Price, R. H. (2007). *Happiness, health, or relationships?*

    Managerial practices and employee well-being tradeoffs. Academy of Management.

Happiness Research Institute. (2017). *Job Satisfaction Index.* Denmark: Krifa's Center of

    knowledge for Job Satisfaction. Retrieved from

    https://docs.wixstatic.com/ugd/928487_f752364b0a43488c8c767532c0de4926.pdf

Hayes, J. E., & Singer, S. J. (2014). Conducting small group research within large, dynamic,

    complex organizations. *Sage research methods cases.*

Helliwell, J. F., Layard, R., & Sachs, J. D. (2018). *World Happiness Report.* Retrieved from

    https://s3.amazonaws.com/happiness-report/2018/WHR_web.pdf

Husain, Z. (2013). Effective communication brings successful organizational change. *The*

    Business & Management Review, 3, 43-50.

IDEO.org. (2015). *The field guide to human-centred design. San Francisco.* Retrieved from

    IDEO.org: http://www.designkit.org/

Kouzes, J. M., & Posner, B. Z. (2012). *The leadership challenge: How to make extraordinary*

    things happen in organizations (5th ed.). San Francisco: A Wiley Brand.

Lewis, S., Passmore, J., & Cantore, S. (2011). *Appreciative inquiry for change management:*

    Using AI to facilitate organizational development. London: Kogan Page.

Lipmanowicz, H., & McCandless, K. (2013). *The suprising power of liberating structures:*

    Simple rules to unleash a culture of innovation. Liberating Structures Press.

Mafini, C., & Dlodlo, N. (2014). The relationship between extrinsic motivation, job satisfaction

    and life satisfaction amongst employees in a public organisation. *SA Journal of Industrial*

    Psychology, 40, 1-13.

McCandless, K., & Lipmanowicz, H. (n.d). *Purpose.* Retrieved from Liberating structures:

    Including and unleashing everyone: www.liberatingstructures.com/purpose/

Newman, D. B., Tay, L., & Diener, E. (2013). *Leisure and Subjective Well-Being: A model of*

    psychological mechanisms as mediating factors. Springer Science+Business Media

    Dordrecht. doi:10.1007/s10902-013-9435-x

Newstrom, J. W. (2002). Making work fun: An important role for managers. *S.A.M. Advanced*

    Management Journal, 67(1), 4-8.

North Vancouver Recreation Commission. (2018). *about us*. Retrieved from

    www.nvrc.ca/about-us

North Vancouver Recreation Commission. (2018). *about us*. Retrieved from NVRC:

    https://www.nvrc.ca/about-us

Owler, K., Morrison, R., & Plester, B. (2010). Does fun work? The complexity of promoting fun

    at work. *Journal of Management & Organization, 16*, 338-352.

Plooy, J. d., & Roodt, G. (2010). Work engagement, burnout and related constructs as predictors

    of turnover intentions. *SA Journal of Industrial Psychology, 36*, 1-13.

Rapaport, R. N. (1970). *Three dilemmas in action reesearch.* Human Relations.

Saldana, J., & Omasta, M. (2018). *Qualitative Research: Analyzing life.* Thousand Oaks: SAGE

    Publications.

Senge, P. M. (1990). *The Fifth Discipline.* New York: Doubleday.

Shaheen, M., Zeba, F., & Mohanty, P. (2017). Can engaged and positive employees delight

    customers? *Advances in Developing Human Resources, 20*, 103-122.

Small, S. A. (1995). Action-oriented research: Models and Methods. *Journal of Marriage and*

    Family.

Statistics Canada. (2016). Retrieved from Statcan:

www12.statcan.gc.ca/census-recensement/2016

Stroh, D. P. (2015). *Systems thinking for social change.* White River Junction, VT: Chelsea

Green Publishing.

Taris, T. W., & Schreurs, P. J. (2009). Well-being and organizational performance: An

organizational-level test of the happy-productive worker hypothesis. *Work & Stress, 23,*

120-136.

Warren, C. (2001). Qualitative interviewing. In Gubrium, J.F., & Holsetein, J.A. *Handbook of*

interview research, 83-102. doi:10.4135/9781412973588

Weisbord, M. R. (2012). *Productive Workplaces; Dignity, meaning, and community in the 21st*

century. San Francisco: Jossey-Bass.

Wright, T. A., Bonett, D. G., & Cropanzano, R. (2007). The moderating role of employee

positive well-being on the relation between job satisfaction and job performance. *Journal*

of Occupational Health Psychology, 12, 93-104.

Appendix A

Letter of Invitation

Dear (Prospective Participant),

I would like to invite you to be part of a research project that I am conducting. This project is part of the requirement for my Master's Degree in Leadership, at Royal Roads University. This project has been approved by the North Vancouver Recreation and Culture Commission, Janet Wallace, and I have been given permission to contact potential participants for this purpose.

The purpose of my research project is to find out how to further enhance the level of happiness staff experience at work and understand how happiness relates to job satisfaction and job performance during change.

Your name was chosen as a prospective participant because you are an employee at the Harry Jerome Recreation Centre employed with the North Vancouver Recreation Commission. This phase of my research project will consist of a Happiness Summit and is estimated to last for 3 hours. The Happiness Summit is scheduled for Thursday, June 21st from 9am – noon in the Mahon Room at Harry Jerome Community Centre.

The attached document contains further information about the study conduct and will enable you to make a fully informed decision on whether or not you wish to participate. Please review this information before responding.

You are not required to participate in this research project. If you do choose to participate, you are free to withdraw prior to the Happiness Summit without prejudice.

I realize that due to our collegial relationship, you may feel compelled to participate in this research project. Please be aware that you are not required to participate and, should you choose to participate, your participation would be entirely voluntary. If you do choose to participate, you are free to withdraw up until the date of the Happiness Summit without prejudice. If you do not wish to participate, simply do not reply to this request. Your decision to not participate will also be maintained in confidence. Your choice will not affect our relationship or your employment status in any way.

Please feel free to contact me at any time should you have additional questions regarding the project and its outcomes. If you would like to participate in my research project, please contact me at:

Name: Jennifer Folkersen

Email: jennifer.folkersen@nvrc.ca

Telephone: **604 808-9939**

Sincerely,

Jennifer Folkersen

Appendix B

Letter of Informed Consent

By signing this form, you agree that you are over the age of 19 and have read the information letter for this study. Your signature states that you are giving your voluntary and informed consent to participate in this project and have data I contribute used in the final report and any other knowledge outputs (articles, conference presentations, newsletters, etc.).

☐   I consent to the audio recording of the Interviews

☐   I consent to have the final report shared with the North Vancouver Recreation Commission staff and for professional purposes and future presentations, provided my identity is not disclosed.

☐   I consent to quotations and excerpts expressed by me through the Happiness Summit be included in this study, provided that my identity is not disclosed

☐   I consent to the material I have contributed to and/or generated including; flipcharts, and notes of my participation in the Happiness Summit be used in this study

☐   I commit to respect the confidential nature of the Happiness Summit by not sharing identifying information about the other participants

Name: (Please Print): _____

Signed: _____

Date: _____

Appendix C

Inquiry Team Member Letter of Agreement

In partial fulfillment of the requirement for a Master of Arts in Leadership Degree at Royal Roads University, Jennifer Folkersen will be conducting an inquiry research study at the North Vancouver Recreation Commission to inquire about enhancing employee happiness through change. The Student's credentials with Royal Roads University can be established by calling Dr. Catherine Etmanski, Director, School of Leadership, at (250) 391-2600 x 4162 or email Catherine.etmanski@RoyalRoads.ca.

Inquiry Team Member Role Description

As a volunteer Inquiry Team Member assisting the Student with this project, your role may include one or more of the following: providing advice on the relevance and wording of questions and letters of invitation, supporting the logistics of the data-gathering methods, including observing, assisting, or facilitating an interview or focus group, taking notes, transcribing, or reviewing analysis of data, to assist the Student and the North Vancouver Recreation and Culture Commission's organizational change process. In the course of this activity, you may be privy to confidential inquiry data.

Confidentiality of Inquiry Data

In compliance with the Royal Roads University Research Ethics Policy, under which this inquiry project is being conducted, all personal identifiers and any other confidential information generated or accessed by the inquiry team advisor will only be used in the performance of the functions of this project and must not be disclosed to anyone other than persons authorized to receive it, both during the inquiry period and beyond it. Recorded information in all formats is covered by this agreement. Personal identifiers include participant names, contact information, personally identifying turns of phrase or comments, and any other personally identifying information.

Bridging Student's Potential or Actual Ethical Conflict

In situations where potential participants in a work setting report directly to the Student, you, as a neutral third party with no supervisory relationship with either the Student or potential participants, may be asked to work closely with the Student to bridge this potential or actual conflict of interest in this study. Such requests may include asking the Inquiry Team Advisor to: send out the letter of invitation to potential participants, receive letters/emails of interest in participation from potential participants, independently make a selection of received participant requests based on criteria you and the Student will have worked out previously, formalize the logistics for the data-gathering method, including contacting the participants about the time and location of the interview or focus group, conduct the interviews (usually 3-5 maximum) or focus group (usually no more than one) with the selected participants (without the Student's presence or knowledge of which participants were chosen) using the protocol and questions worked out previously with the Student, and producing written transcripts of the interviews or focus groups with all personal identifiers removed before the transcripts are brought back to the Student for the data analysis phase of the study.

This strategy means that potential participants with a direct reporting relationship will be assured they can confidentially turn down the participation request from their supervisor (the Student), as this process conceals from the Student which potential participants chose not to participate or simply were not selected by you, the third party, because they were out of the selection criteria range (they might have been a participant request coming after the number of participants sought, for example, interview request number 6 when only 5 participants are sought, or focus group request number 10 when up to 9 participants would be selected for a focus group). Inquiry Team members asked to take on such 3rd party duties in this study will be under the direction of the Student and will be fully briefed by the Student as to how this process will work, including specific expectations, and the methods to be employed in conducting the elements of the inquiry with the Student's direct reports, and will be given every support possible by the Student, except where such support would reveal the identities of the actual participants.

Personal information will be collected, recorded, corrected, accessed, altered, used, disclosed, retained, secured and destroyed as directed by the Student, under direction of the Royal Roads Academic Supervisor.

Inquiry Team Members who are uncertain whether any information they may wish to share about the project they are working on is personal or confidential will verify this with Jennifer Folkersen, the Student.

Statement of Informed Consent:

I have read and understand this agreement.

_____   _____

Name (Please Print)   Signature   Date

Appendix D

Research Question: How might we increase happiness in the workplace while experiencing

organizational change?

Sub question: What changes need to be made to raise your level of happiness in the

workplace?

Sub question: What is our potential we still need to discover?

Sub question: What would you imagine this team would look like if the level of

happiness and engagement increased?

Sub question: What is your current level of happiness at work?

Sub question: How might change affect our levels of happiness at work?

Sub question: What might we create to support our teams happiness at work?

Appendix E

Interview/Happiness Summit Plan

A ½ day Happiness Summit using an approach of appreciative inquiry through a design thinking model of Inspiration and Ideation. For the purpose of this project, the Implementation and Sharing the Story will be done outside of this research project.

Inspiration Phase

The inspiration phase will include 2 phases: Interviews and a Happiness Summit:

(1) 3- 30-minute interviews to better understand the hopes of the team. These interviews will be aimed at 3 program coordinators, who work in various areas (Fitness, Access and Aquatics). I will ask the participants to leave out any names or identifying information in questions d – g.

Interview questions:

(1) How happy are you generally when you come to work?

(2) What are some of the things that affect your happiness at work?

(3) When changes happen at work, how does this affect your happiness?

(4) Can you tell me about a situation or scenario where you felt really happy at work?

(5) What was it about that scenario that increased your level of happiness?

(6) Can you tell me about a situation or scenario where you felt less than happy at work

(7) What was it about that scenario that decreased your level of happiness?

Happiness Summit:

Inspiration Phase

Activity 1: Collage exercise

Purpose: To identify group values and themes and see if anything unexpected appears to

further evaluate. I will provide a series of photo cards for participants to look

through and choose which fits in regard to the prompts listed below.

Prompt: Pick 1 picture that resonates with you when thinking about happiness at work

Report out: Have one person write out describing words on post its

Prompt: Pick 1 picture that resonates with you to describe how you feel when large

organizational changes take effect at work

Report out: Have one person write out describing words on post its

Ideation Phase

Activity 2: Top 5

Have groups at their tables, find the Top 5 themes from collage exercise. Take

post-its from Activity 1 and put them all on the wall, have the group sort through,

find themes and categorize based on top emerging themes.

Activity 3: Brainstorm

From theme exercise, brainstorm ways to create or enhance happiness at work by

writing down big ideas on flip chart paper.

Report out

Activity 4: Bundle Ideas

Start clustering brainstorm ideas into actionable solutions by writing on flip chart paper

Report out and from this ask for participants to make conclusions based on what they have heard. This member checking will ensure validity of data.

Once the happiness summit is complete, I will go through a series of theming and categorizing based on what was presented with my inquiry team to see if there is anything else surprising that came from the data.

Implementation

Activity 5:   Dotmocracy

Have group take 3 sticky dots and choose their top 3 actionable solutions for implementation

Appendix F

Information Letter

My name is Jennifer Folkersen, and this research project is part of the requirement for a Master of Arts in Leadership at Royal Roads University. My credentials with Royal Roads University can be established by contacting Dr. Catherine Etmanski, Director, School of Leadership Studies: Catherine.etmanski@RoyalRoads.ca or 250 391-2600 ext. 4162.

Purpose of the study and sponsoring organization

The purpose of my research project is to find out how to further enhance the level of happiness staff experience at work and understand how happiness relates to job satisfaction and job performance while going through organizational change. The sponsoring organization for this study is the North Vancouver Recreation and Culture Commission.

Your participation and how information will be collected

The research will consist of a ½ day Happiness Summit, where I will use an approach to research called Design Thinking. Design Thinking is a human centered approach to creating big ideas about what is possible. Phases of design thinking include gathering inspiration, generating ideas, making those ideas tangible and then sharing the story. I'll be doing this by using simple rules that will include everyone through lively activities that will unleash everyone to create happiness innovation for the future. The data will be collected by a graphic recorder in a large picture format.

Benefits and risks to participation

Using a group format, the process is expected to create new ideas and team collaboration that will enhance issues relevant to the North Vancouver Recreation and Culture Commission, as well the project should address a meaningful purpose for the participants and the organization. New knowledge will be gained and may lead to positive change.

As the project will be completed through a group format, information presented will not be anonymous, as the group will consist of peers. However, the positive nature of the project should not pose any risk to the participants or the organization.

Inquiry team

My inquiry team consists of Derek Lowe, MA.

Real or Perceived Conflict of Interest

As I am a team member of the study participants, I do not expect there to be any real or perceived conflict of interest. The team at all levels works together in partnership on many programs and services for the benefit of the community. If participants are feeling unable to express themselves freely in this type of group setting, they are welcome to follow up with myself. I disclose this information here so that you can make a fully informed decision on whether or not to participate in this study.

Confidentiality, security of data, and retention period

I will work to protect your privacy throughout this study. All information I collect will be maintained in confidence with hard copies (e.g., consent forms) stored in a locked filing cabinet in my home office. Information will be recorded in hand-written format and/or audio recorded

and where appropriate, summarized, in anonymous format, in the body of the final report. At no

time, will any specific comments be attributed to any individual unless specific agreement has

been obtained beforehand. All documentation will be kept strictly confidential. Due to the

nature of the group method, it is not possible to keep identities of the participants anonymous

from the researcher, facilitator, or other participants. I will ask participants to respect the

confidential nature of the research by not sharing names or identifying comments outside of the

group.

Sharing results

In addition to submitting my final report to Royal Roads University in partial fulfillment for a

Master of Arts in Leadership, I will also be sharing my research findings with the North

Vancouver Recreation and Culture Commission. My research report will be presented to the

Commission and each research participant will receive a copy.

Procedure for withdrawing from the study

Participants may withdraw from the study prior to the Happiness Summit by contacting myself,

the researcher, Jennifer Folkersen at Jennifer.folkersen@nvrc.ca or by calling 604 808-9939.

Due to the nature of the group format, participant data collected during the Happiness Summit

may not be withdrawn.

You are not required to participate in this research project. By replying directly to the email

request for participation, you indicate that you have read and understand the information above

and give your free and informed consent to participate in this project.

Please keep a copy of this information letter for your records.

Appendix G Milestone Timeline for ELP Deliverables			
Milestone	Date shared on Moodle for peer review	Target Completion Date	Date Completed/to be completed
Proposal Complete (including any changes requested by 640 faculty advisor)	April 12	March 28	March 28
Team Charter & ELP Pod Confidentiality Agreement	April 1	April 1	April 1
Letter of Agreement with ELP Partner signed, scanned, and uploaded		April 20	April 22
REB Request for Ethical Review and Compliance Agreement (if required) submitted to ELP Pod Supervisor. (Students are asked to budget approximately one month to complete the REB approval process once ELP Pod Supervisors have submitted their request to the Research Ethics office.)		April 22	April 29
First Deliverable Complete and posted to Moodle (Note: this will vary depending on the nature of your ELP. For example, this could be first data collection method or first round of engagement with stakeholders) Happiness Summit – initial thoughts and reflections		May 31	May 31
Second Deliverable Complete and posted to Moodle as per your ELP Happiness Summit – Data analysis and summary of key points		June 30	June 30
Share Design Thinking plan and liberating structures with Pod	Around June 15	June 30	June 30
Literature review and completion		June 30	June 30
First draft of findings, conclusions, limitations		June 30	June 30
Share research findings and highlights with POD	Around July 10	July 10	July 10
First draft of recommendations and implications		July 15	July 15
First draft of ELP summary		July 30	July 30
Updated proposal to create sections of final report: • Focus and framing		May 1 – Aug 15	

• Significance of the project • Relevant literature • Engaged approach • References Appendices			
Final Draft ELP Report Complete for ELP Pod Supervisor's review		Aug 15	Aug 15
Full Project to ELP Pod Supervisor for Approval		Aug 26	Aug 26
Share learnings with POD "What I know now, v. what I knew then"	1st week of Sept	1st week of Sept	1st week of Sept
Student sends final report and other Knowledge Product(s) to Partner and provides them the Partner Evaluation survey link		Sept 7	Sept 7
Draft of ELP Reflection to ELP Pod Supervisor's review		Sept 14	Sept 14
ELP Reflection Complete		Sept 16	Sept 16

www.ingramcontent.com/pod-product-compliance
Lightning Source LLC
Chambersburg PA
CBHW081302180526
45170CB00007B/2533